In a volatile and uncerta
world where the pace of
life is faster than it has
ever been, it is becomin
increasingly important
to be able to think on
your feet and adapt and
respond with greater
speed and ease.

Behavioural agility is
essentially about tapping
into your dynamic
capability so that you can
thrive through challenging
and changing times.

This bite sized book will offer simple and practical
advice that will help you to:

✓   Respond and adapt better and quicker to change

✓   Be more self aware, confident and authentic

✓   Innovate through curiosity and collaboration

✓   Let go of things that hinder your progress

✓   Build personal resilience through balance and
     pace

We are living in a VUCA world

A technological revolution is taking place that will fundamentally change the way we live, work, and relate to one another. The scale, scope, complexity and transformation will be unlike anything humankind has experienced before. Exactly how it will unfold, and the impact it will have, is still unclear. The only certainty is that it will be disruptive!

VUCA is an acronym that derives from military vocabulary and reflects the volatility, uncertainty, complexity and ambiguity of general conditions and situations in which we may well find ourselves.

VUCA Prime

An effective "VUCA counterweight" framework has been developed by Bob Johansen, distinguished fellow at the Institute for the Future, and this is known as VUCA PRIME.

Being able to positively turn VUCA around by cultivating vision, understanding, clarity and agility is key to creating an environment where people can flourish in turbulent times.

The world of work is changing and there is a growing need for a more agile approach to the way organisations operate.

Agile working is where an organisation empowers its people to work where, when and how they choose with maximum flexibility and minimum constraints. Communications and information technology are pivotal in making this happen.

The idea behind this approach is to create a more responsive, efficient and effective organisation, which can keep up with the pace of innovation, improve business performance and increase customer satisfaction.

Behavioural agility is about your ability to adjust and flex your behaviour by employing different facets of emotional intelligence. It will require you to adopt a growth mindset and be open to new learning and possibilities.

This will require you to learn, unlearn and relearn new ways of doing things, step out of your comfort zone and feel comfortable with uncertainty. Cultivating a deep desire to tap into your dynamic capability and exploring your potential is essential.

By being adaptable to change, confident, curious and courageous, nimble and resilient you will be fit for the future and be able to fully embrace the new developments of the 21st century.

Becoming is better than being

Carol S Dweck

The illiterate of the 21st Century
are not those who cannot read
and write but those who cannot
learn, unlearn and relearn

Alvin Toffler

A ...Adaptable

G ...Genuine

I ...Innovative

L ...Light

E ...Enduring

The AGILE model

This behavioural model, developed by The Learning Architect, describes 5 key components that are fundamental to behavioural agility:

A is about being adaptable, so that you can be open, flexible and responsive around change

G is about being genuine, so that you operate with authenticity and achieve a greater level of self-confidence and purpose

I is about being innovative, so that you can adopt a curious mindset and are prepared to explore new ways of doing things

L is about being light and letting go of anything that may hinder your progress and responsiveness

E is about being enduring so that you are balanced, well-paced, healthy and resilient

A.G.I.L.E. – Adaptable

So the first component in the acronym of agile is about "adaptability".

As far as this is concerned the words of Charles Darwin resonate more poignantly than ever:

It is not the strongest of the species that survives, nor the most intelligent, but rather the one most adaptable to change.

Sometimes it may feel that as soon as you adapt to one set of circumstances it's all change again! That, however, is evolution and there is no progress without change.

Ancient wisdom teaches us that the secret to change is to focus your energy, not on fighting the old, but on building the new.

The biggest obstacle to being agile can be your attitude towards change.

If you find yourself resistant to change then the chances are that you will be setting yourself up for a tough time. Very often in life you may experience change that you don't like or even understand and it may well be that there is nothing you can do to stop it.

On occasions you may dig your heels in, however there comes a point where the wave of change is a lot stronger than you are capable of conquering. In this situation real intelligence teaches you that whilst you may not be able to change the situation you can choose your response.

Adapting your mindset will be the most powerful response and focusing on the positive outcomes and how you can influence those changes will be a far more intentional use of your energy than resistance.

How to be adaptable

Tip one – Appreciate that change is inevitable and if it is something that you can't do anything about then adjust your attitude to respond more openly and positively.

Tip two – Understand that every experience in your life, whether it is good or bad, will bring a valuable lesson with it. Very often a change that you may see initially as problematic may well turn into an opportunity, or at least teach you something you didn't know before which will help you in the future.

Tip three – Acceptance is a big part of being able to be adaptable. Whilst you may like to be in control and be the master of your own destiny, holding on too tightly can indeed deplete your energy resources. Being able to accept your circumstances rather than fight them will give you more strength and control in the long term.

TOP
3
TIPS

Change is not merely
necessary to life
- it is life

Alvin Toffler

A.G.I.L.E. – Genuine

The second component of the AGILE acronym is about being *genuine*.

Something important to establish here is that *you were not born to be perfect, you were born to be real.*

In a world that is dominated by social media, sometimes it can be a struggle to determine the real self from the selectively designed image of the ideal self. Although you will want to project yourself in the best possible light, it is important that you never lose sight of who you really are.

We are all people in progress and there will always be aspects of yourself that can be worked on and improved. Having a high level of self-awareness can improve self-esteem and confidence. Self-confidence will help you to trust your own responses, which is a big part of being agile and making decisions.

Having a good understanding of your strengths and limitations, your hopes and vulnerabilities is important.

Getting things wrong is part of the human condition. This can be challenging at times because education doesn't always equip us with how to deal with mistakes because so much focus is on getting it right and success.

It is worth pondering the following question:

How did *you* learn some of the most valuable lessons in your life?

Was it when everything went right and worked out well, or was it when you made a mistake and got it wrong?

Learning from your mistakes can be some of the most important stepping-stones in shaping your dynamic capability; so don't be afraid to trip up from time to time.

Being *genuine* with a strong sense of self-belief will also help you to be confident about exploring your true potential and greater purpose.

How to be genuine

Tip one – Understand that, for every strength, you will have a counterpart limitation and that is the cost/opportunity of life. Capitalising on your strengths and being mindful of your limitations will equip you to be more self-aware and improve your personal intelligence.

Tip two – It's OK to get it wrong sometimes. It may well be that if you are not making mistakes then you are not actually doing anything new and doers do get it wrong from time to time!

Tip three – Believe in yourself and your ability. Sometimes you may be your harshest critic and give yourself a hard time by comparing yourself to other people or trying to be something other than who you really are. Remember originals have the greatest value and exploring your true purpose is the most potent motivator.

TOP
3
TIPS

The most inspiring role model you can ever have, is an improved version of yourself.

Liggy Webb

A.G.I.L.E. – Innovative

The third component of the AGILE acronym is about being innovative.

Increasingly in a world where there is less security and more uncertainty and ambiguity, it is important to explore ways of doings things differently.

As the saying goes – *If you always do what you have always done – you will always get what you have always got.* So, if you want different outcomes you have to be prepared to explore and experiment.

Being curious is the engine of innovation and exploring new ways of doing things is really important for your cognitive function, as well as keeping things interesting, fresh and exciting.

In the pioneering 21st century, tried and tested methods of what may have been appropriate yesterday may not be relevant and appropriate for the working conditions of today and tomorrow. To keep a competitive edge it is really important to innovate and explore new ways of doing things.

There is, of course, a certain risk attached to innovation, which very often can create limitation because it is easier to stay within a secure comfort zone. The issue with this is that doing what we perceive is within our comfort zone right now may be the biggest risk for future success.

Being curious and collaborating with others can help you to open the door to a whole host of exciting new opportunities and experiences.

How to be innovative

Tip one – Be open-minded about exploring new ways of doing things. It is really useful to generate new ideas and investigating new approaches may well save you time in the long term and deliver much better results.

Tip two – Acknowledge that in a world that is very much geared to keeping things fresh and interesting there is more of a demand to reinvent and reinvigorate. Sometimes innovation doesn't mean radical change; it may be more about revitalising what you already have.

Tip three – Develop a good set of creative tools that will assist you in exploring new options and avenues.

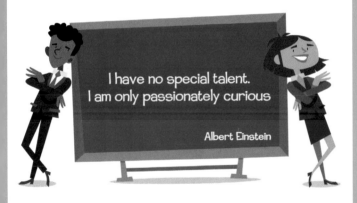

I have no special talent.
I am only passionately curious

Albert Einstein

A.G.I.L.E. – Light

The fourth component of the agile acronym is about being light.

Agility requires you to think and respond quickly so that your approach is relevant to the current circumstances.

It isn't however OK running about like a headless chicken and multi-tasking at breakneck speed, it is about being sharper and more focused. If our personal systems are overcomplicated and our minds are overwhelmed and cluttered, it is impossible to navigate some of the complexity that is rife.

Being light on your feet and a nimble thinker will help you to be more responsive.

A great deal of what we do we do on autopilot. This means we have collected behavioural habits through our lifetimes and much of what we do we do without really thinking about it. It is important to take time to examine those habits and to decide how helpful they are. It may well be that some of those habits are restrictive and indeed unnecessary baggage that can slow you down and hinder your progress.

To be a nimble thinker one of the most important things is to be able to distil complexity and make things as simple and straightforward as possible.

Overloading yourself with too much unnecessary baggage will slow you down and hinder your ability to be agile.

How to be light

Tip one – Review everything you do and look at ways to simplify any processes that you have in place. Anything that feels complicated and overly time-consuming needs to be examined and adapted and even eliminated if appropriate.

Tip two – Let go of the past. Whenever you find yourself ruminating over things that have happened in an unhelpful or negative way, you need to draw a line and move on! Use the past as a useful database, not as a dwelling place!

Tip three – Avoid obsessing about things that worry you about the future. If you do this it will drag you down and make you feel heavy. Conduct a risk assessment and then do a list of cons and pros. By writing down the cons first you can then flip it over and focus on the pros and the hope you have. This approach will keep you feeling less weighed down by anxiety and worry and more hopeful and light about the future.

TOP
3
TIPS

Being light minded will help
you to create clarity and
be a nimble thinker

Liggy Webb

A.G.I.L.E. – Enduring

The final component of the AGILE acronym is about being enduring.

Behavioural agility is very much about endurance and building personal resilience by being balanced, well-paced and resilient.

With some of the pressures that modern life can put you under there is a greater need than ever to develop an inner strength so that you can bounce back ready for the next challenge. Looking after yourself, avoiding burnout by cultivating healthy habits and finding a happy balance between home and work is so important.

Resilience is a term that is being used more and more. There is an increasing need to be able to bounce through adversity and overcome setbacks by taking personal responsibility and being agile and positive.

Self-care and a heightened awareness of your stress levels and physical and mental well-being is of paramount importance.

Establishing healthy habits, boundaries and moments of sanctuary will help you stay ignited and conserve valuable energy.

Endurance is about cultivating strength and stamina so that you can pace yourself well and enjoy the journey.

The 3 Pillars of Resilience

How to be enduring

Tip one – Take responsibility for everything that happens to you in your life. It is easy to fall into the trap of blaming other people. The most empowering statement is to say – *I am responsible for everything that happens to me in my life because I can choose how I respond.*

Tip two – Before you act, consider the effect it will have. Everything you do and the choices you make will bear longer-term consequences.

Tip three – Acknowledge that endurance is not just about bearing difficult situations. Endurance is about cultivating strength and stamina so you can go at a pace that works well for you.

Catch the life with the agility of a dog trying to get a hold of the flying Frisbee

Mehmet Murat ildan

It is not the strongest of the species that survives, nor the most intelligent. It is the one that is most adaptable to change.

Charles Darwin

34